The Picture that Mom Drew

written and illustrated by
Kathy Mallat

written and photo-illustrated by
Bruce McMillan

WALKER AND COMPANY ✸ NEW YORK

"This is our mom.

This is the paper
used for the picture
that Mom drew.

These are the **colors**

that brightened the paper

used for the picture

that Mom drew.

These are some lines

sketched with the colors

that brightened the paper

used for the picture

that Mom drew.

These are some shapes

drawn with the l i n e s

sketched with the colors

that brightened the paper

used for the picture

that Mom drew.

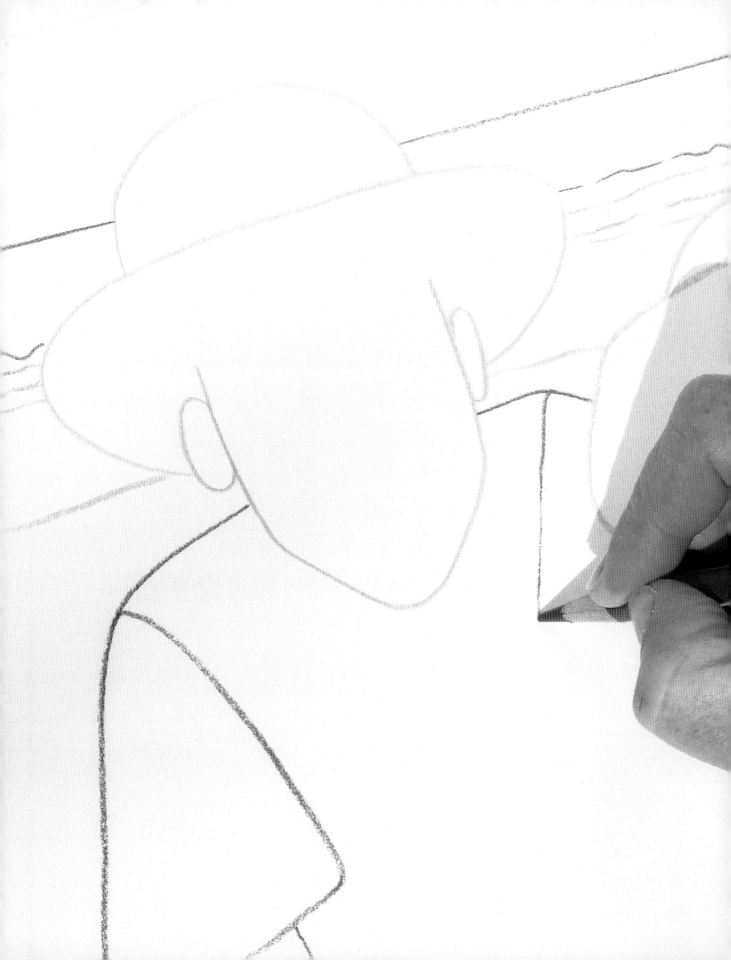

These are some forms

molded from the shapes

drawn with the l i n e s

sketched with the colors

that brightened the paper

used for the picture

that Mom drew.

These are some **shades**

layered over the **forms**

molded from the shapes

drawn with the l i n e s

sketched with the **colors**

that brightened the paper

used for the picture

that Mom drew.

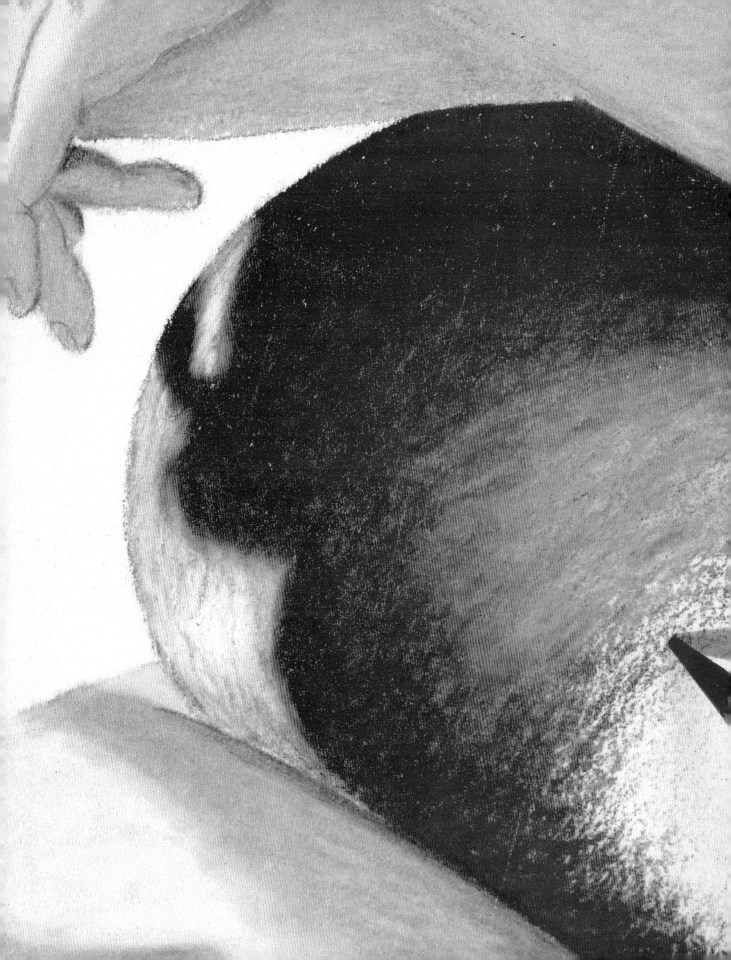

These are some **patterns**

enhanced by the **shades**

layered over the **forms**

molded from the shapes

drawn with the l i n e s

sketched with the **colors**

that brightened the paper

used for the picture

that Mom drew.

These are some **textures**

next to the **patterns**

enhanced by the **shades**

layered over the **forms**

molded from the **shapes**

drawn with the <u>l i n e s</u>

sketched with the **colors**

that brightened the paper

used for the picture

that Mom drew, and…

this is the picture

that Mom drew."

The Elements of Art that Mom Used

Colors are reflected light waves. Substances that reflect colors–pigments–are used to make colored pencils, paints, and even the inks used to print this book.

The **primary colors** are red, blue, and yellow.

The **secondary colors** are purple, green, and orange. They are made by mixing two primary colors together. Red and blue make purple. Blue and yellow make green. Red and yellow make orange.

Warm colors, such as reds, yellows, or oranges, sometimes evoke a feeling of warmth.

Cool colors, such as blues, greens, or violets, sometimes evoke a feeling of cold.

Lines are long narrow marks.

Shapes are areas with an outline, such as circles, squares, rectangles, and triangles, that have only two dimensions, height and width.

Forms are three dimensional spaces with an outline, such as spheres, cylinders, cubes, and pyramids, that have height, width, and depth.

Shades are gradual changes of a color from dark to light.

Patterns are a rhythmic repetition of lines, shapes, forms, or colors.

Textures show the way surfaces feel, such as smooth, rough, or bumpy.

For my dad, David W. Sherburne —K.M.
For my high school art teacher, Marylyn Wentworth —B.M.

A Note from the Authors

The two girls in the picture, Erin and her younger sister, Meghan, are the daughters of Kathy and Steve Mallat. They were photographed at a secluded coastal beach in southern Maine. Kathy's drawings were made using Berol Prismacolor colored pencils on Strathmore 500 Series Bristol Board paper. Bruce's photographs were made using a Nikon F4 camera with an MF23 back set to bracket exposures, and a 105 mm f 2.8 micro Nikon lens, either with no filter, a light blue filter, or polarizing filter. An aluminum foil reflector for fill light was used in all photos. The book was designed by Bruce, using Optima for text type, and both Arab Brush and a redrawn Gill Sans for display type.

Kathy Mallat   Bruce McMillan

First published in the United States of America in 1997
by Walker Publishing Company, Inc.

Published simultaneously in Canada by
Thomas Allen & Son Canada,
Limited, Markham, Ontario

Library of Congress Cataloging-in-Publication Data
Mallat, Kathy.
The picture that Mom drew/written and illustrated by Kathy Mallat;
written and photo-illustrated by Bruce McMillan.   p. cm.
Summary: Introduces the seven basic elements of art by using
colored pencils to add colors, lines, shapes, forms, shades,
patterns, and textures one at a time to a piece of paper.
ISBN 0-8027-8617-0 (hardcover: alk. paper).
—ISBN 0-8027-8618-9 (reinforced: alk. paper)
1. Colored pencil drawing—Technique—Juvenile literature.
[1. Colored pencil drawing—Technique. 2. Drawing—Technique.]
I. McMillan, Bruce. II. Title.
NC892.M35 1997 741.2'4—DC20 96-30165 CIP AC

Printed in Hong Kong

2 4 6 8 10 9 7 5 3 1

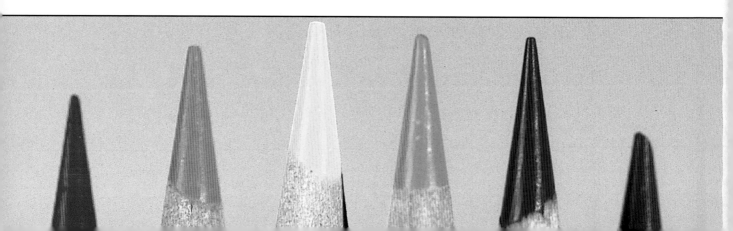